MW00941671

Iowa Nice

Genial Jokes for a Gentle People

To Merle best wishes and thanks!
Ron Wiggins

"Polishing Iowa's Image"

by Ron Wiggins

From the author of

The First Book of Last Times and *Weird Snacks*

www.iowanice.com

In memory of Pearl Whyte,
exemplary Iowan.

To the people of Iowa, good sports all,
and by good sports I mean folks who can lose
at Monopoly to a gloater with hotels on Boardwalk and Park
Place and not want to shove a tiny choo-choo up somebody's
nose.

Special thanks to Pat Crowley for illustrations
and spot art.

patcrowleyspenheads.blogspot.com

FOREWORD

Mike Dalton, author of "The North Dakota Joke Book," observed "that there is a universal need to tell a joke at someone else's expense."

I hope he's wrong.

Laughing at someone else's expense is easy. Laughing at someone else's profit, now that's tough. Try making someone the beneficiary of a joke instead of the butt, and see how that registers on the laugh-o-meter.

And yet this is what I have attempted – finding humor in virtue. My premise is that Iowans are such wholesome, down to earth people that they are hilarious – and don't know it. "Iowa Nice – *Genial Jokes for a Gentle People*" peers deep into the creamy nougaty soul of the Iowan citizenry and shows us a reflection of what the rest of us would be like if we hadn't skipped so much Sunday school.

I guess I'm the first outsider to write a book telling Iowans how great they are. I'm not sure how they'll take that, Iowans being a pretty modest bunch.

Modest? Iowan nudists wear Groucho nose glasses.

And unassuming? Iowans won't even assume a 4.5 percent mortgage unless it's a 30-year fixed and the bank throws in a toaster.

As for straight-dealing - when an Iowan closes a savings account, the bank returns the money in the same knotted handkerchief.

Yes, I'm joking, but on the square. I ladle it on pretty thick. "Iowa Nice", I like to think, inflates without puffing up; toasts without roasting; and teases without needling. And if you like the idea of people being made fun of for their good qualities, you're about to see how that works.

Warning: I threw in a few jokes that mock, belittle, degrade, insult and make fun of other states including my own beloved Florida. These serve as bad examples. You are not meant to laugh.

Ron Wiggins, Big Iowa Fan

SKIPPED THE FOREWORD, DID YOU?

Yes, I understand. Jokes now, and easy on the palaver. Patience. I cannot overstress here that the whole idea of "Iowa Nice" is to turn the insult joke inside out; to exalt, never to degrade.

These are jokes and gentle observations meant to hold Iowa and Iowans aloft so that the rest of us can choose to a) admire them, b) gnaw out our livers with envy, or c) come up with more jokes to celebrate Iowa for being chock full of squeaky clean down home values.

Where's the fun in that?

Remember fifth grade? Remember how the girls begged the boys to chase down the cutest boy and hold him down so the girls could kiss him? Remember how that lucky kid wasn't that hard to catch and how unconvincing a fight he put up when the kissing squad descended upon him to do their filthy work?

Well, I've got 49 states, including my own – Florida – that I invite to pin Iowans down to their fragrant, loamy earth and tickle them! Now give them some sugar. I'll hold them down. Look, they're not even pretending to struggle. Pile on everybody! They love it!

Q: Are Iowans just naturally a cut above or is there some kind of divine favoritism involved?
A: Favoritism. While the rest of us are dealing with Saint Peter, Iowans pick up their passes at the Will Call window.

I figure it's time that I, a seasoned journalist, blew the whole beautiful lid off Iowa's clean little secret:

They're nice as pie.

Q: How did the Iowan know he was in a cheap Chinese restaurant?
A: When he asked for a napkin, the waiter brought him a box of silk worms and a whip.

Q: How does a diner know when he or she has over-tipped an Iowa waitress?
A: She chases him down the street waving money.

Q: How does a **South Dakotan** know when he's over-tipped?
A: The cow helps him back over the fence with her horns.

Q: How does a **Canadian** know he's over-tipped?
A: You've got to be kidding.

Q: Why are Iowans a lot smarter than **Floridians**?
A: Iowans have cow pie throwing contests. Floridians have cow pie catching contests.

Q: What makes an Iowan happy?
A: When it's her turn to hold the puppy.

Q: What makes her even happier?
A: Everybody calls the puppy and the puppy comes to her.

Q: Why are Iowans so careful to count their change?
A: They don't want the cashier to come up short at the end of the shift.

Q: When are Iowans a little *too* law abiding?
A: They stop at yield signs and jump out with their hands up. Oops, sorry, that was a **New Jersey** joke.

Q: Why do Iowans have more fun than **Minnesotans**?
A: When Minnesotans see a waxed floor they think of yellow wax build-up. When Iowans see a waxed floor they kick off their shoes and slide in their socks.

Q: How do we know Iowans get a bit more from everyday experiences than the rest of us?
A: Before popping the stick of Juicy Fruit into their mouths, they sniff the wrapper for its bouquet.

WHAT'S THAT IN YOUR MOUTH?

Teachers know better than to ask a gum chewer, "Did you bring enough for everybody?" because the kid will be up and out of his seat and handing out 30 sticks of Bazooka.

Iowans won't consult the Whitman's chocolates diagram because if you know what you're getting, that would mean that Forrest Gump's mother was wrong, that life is *not* like a box of chocolates.

In fact, the meanest thing Iowans ever do is switch the chocolates around so that only they know where the caramels are. Then they switch them back because they can't handle the guilt.

Iowans slump in their seats at the picture show. Not because they have bad posture, but so the person in back of them can see.

Few Iowans send hate mail, but those that do can't help themselves and close with xoxoxo.

Speaking of letters, Iowans not only dot their i's and cross their t's, but they mind their p's and q's and mothers.

Iowans never pick at it, and, of course, it does get well.

Iowans with domestic help straighten up the house and dust on Wednesday because the cleaning gal comes on Thursday.

Iowans not only burp their Tupperware, they walk it for five minutes before tucking it in.

Iowans may wear out their invitations, but never their welcome.

Q: How do you make an Iowan blush?
A: Just say "I see London, I see France..."

Iowa men get their wives feeling smoochy by wiping down the kitchen, taking out the garbage without being asked, and saying when they come back into the house, "Honey, I've turned my cap around in case somebody beautiful wants to kiss me."

Q: Why do some educators wonder if Iowa schools put too much stress on agriculture?
A: Report cards have a place for "Farms well with others."

Now that you have a much better idea of what you're in for, it's time to go back 30 years and see the column that gave me the concept of Iowa as a place where folks led such placid lives that any little thing could make their day.

BIRTH OF THE IOWA JOKE:
THE SHOT THAT WAS HEARD
CLEAN TO DES MOINES

Way back in the mists of time, when Jimmy Carter was try-ing to get elected for a second term, and I was writing a local column for *The Palm Beach Post*, I teased Iowa in a way that some Iowans got a big kick out of and others found - well, let's just say there was pouting.

Transplanted Iowans living in South Florida weren't the only Hawkeyes to see that first round of Iowa jokes. My commentary was picked up by *The Des Moines Register* which ran the whole article under this editorial intro:

"The image of Iowa held by outsiders sometimes leaves us shaking our heads in bewilderment. The following column of 'Iowa jokes' by Ron Wiggins of The Palm Beach Post gives one outsider's view of life in our state. Well, at least he realizes we can take a joke."

WHAT? IOWANS EXCITED BY
JIMMY CARTER?

By Ron Wiggins

Palm Beach, FL – When I read in the paper the other day that a "Visit by Carter Turns Iowans On," my first thought was that the future President had revealed himself as Planter's "Mr. Peanut". Nope. Nor did the Georgia peanut farmer pop wheelies on a tractor. Some particle of pure Jimmy Carter charisma, a glint of teeth and a wave of hand- was at work here. That and the fact that Iowans have very low excitement thresholds.

Of course Iowans were excited by Carter. Iowans can find the fun in practically anything. There are still Iowans who run out and point at the sky saying, "Look! An airplane!"

Female Iowans have disturbing dreams about Lawrence Welk. Male Iowans clip Betty Furness out of the refrigerator ads for their workshop pinups.

Iowans satisfy their wanderlust by going to Nebraska.

When Iowans dine out they got to a hospital cafeteria on tapioca day. Iowa is the only state where there's a demand for gray food coloring.

An Iowan's idea of bucking the system is to open the milk carton from the wrong side. Most towns in Iowa are so small that the telephone book has a yellow paragraph.

An Iowan woman diabolically murdered her wealthy aunt, an elderly heart patient, by removing the labels from her soup cans. The excitement of opening the mystery cans did her in.

Most people who wonder what ever happened to Tab Hunter live in Iowa.

What Iowans lack as trend setters they make up for in thrift. The Des Moines Municipal Zoo opened with one animal: a pig that was master of 1,000 disguises.

Playboy Magazine keeps getting the same racy joke from sixth grade boys with Iowa ZIP Codes:

Q: What did the disc harrow say to the tractor?
A: Pull me closer John-Deere

Iowans time their trips to the bathroom so they don't miss the Sanka commercial. Highly optimistic Iowans live in a state of perpetual excitement knowing they may already be a Publisher's Clearing House winner.

In fact, when they get mail addressed to occupant, they cry out, "That's me!"

Not that Iowans are wanting for excitement, but they have been known to drive 30 miles to town to see if Penney's has changed the window display.

No Iowan has been to New York City since 1951 when it was widely believed they would be dragged into the Stork Club, forced to mambo, and charged $10 for a cup of coffee.

Say what you will about Iowans, they do have a sense of humor and can take a joke, something you can't always say about folks from other states. Scratch a Southerner and you'll find a rebel. Scratch a New Yorker and he'll sue. Scratch a Nebraskan and he'll get his tetanus booster. Scratch an Iowan and he'll say "Higher and to the left."

Iowan kids are right out of *Ozzie and Harriet* and *Father Knows Best*. You talk about nice kids – they're in bed sound asleep at 8 p.m. except on Monday nights when they beg to stay up and watch the spin cycle.

I Get My Comeuppance

OK, that was it – my first foray into innocent if not entirely flattering teasing of Iowans - and while sorry don't feed the bulldog as Gramps used to say on the original "Lassie", some of those jokes did have the whiff of hayseed about them, and I am sorry. Retribution was prompt and savage.

I first heard from a Cedar Rapids radio jock who called me with a couple of retaliatory Florida jokes that served me right.

"Florida has so many old people that the smoke alarms are set to go off a day early."

"Floridians are so cheap that their massage parlors are all self-serve."

Now, that's funny. Even funnier was the response I got from fellow scrivener, Donald Kaul of *The Des Moines Register,* in his "Over the Coffee" column:

The Joke's on You Palm Beach
By Donald Kaul

Des Moines, IA — I was at my desk playing Solitaire Chutes and Ladders when my telephone rang. It was my boss, Mr. Big.

"Don," he said, "Iowa is in danger of becoming the laughing-stock of the country."

"Why? Is the legislature going back into session?"

"Worse than that. A columnist has just written a piece filled with Iowa jokes. We printed it on the front page of the *Register* last week:

"Iowa jokes?"

"Yes, he said that male Iowans have sexual fantasies about Betty Furness, the refrigerator ad lady."

"That's a smutty thing to spread around."

"He said that when Iowans dine out, they go to hospital cafeterias on tapioca day and that Iowa is the only state with a demand for gray food coloring."

"Those aren't bad jokes, actually."

"An Iowan's idea of bucking the system is to open the milk carton from the wrong side," he said, and they time their trips to the bathroom so they don't miss the Sanka commercial.

According to this guy, the Des Moines Municipal Zoo has only one animal: a pig who is the master of a thousand disguises."

"That's pretty clever stuff, chief. Where's this columnist from? New York? Chicago? L.A.?"

"His name is Ron Wiggins and he writes for *The Palm Beach Post* in Florida."

"Wait a minute. This guy lives in Palm Beach and he's putting down Iowa? What nerve! Iowa is an environmental disco compared to Palm Beach."

"Is that so?"

"Definitely. Palm Beach is where rich people go to escape civilization in the privacy of their own homes. It's an island connected to the mainland by two draw bridges. They're having a fight right now over whether to make visitors pay a toll to enter the place.

"Say what you will about Des Moines, at least we don't charge admission."

"Living in Palm Beach is the moral equivalent of cutting in line. People there think the greatest benefit of a free democratic society is the restrictive-housing covenant. To them, a *nouveau riche* is anyone whose grandfather worked. In Palm Beach, it's considered a mixed marriage when you marry someone who isn't a second cousin.

"How rich are people in Palm Beach?"

"Very. They hire people to laugh for them. They think we can solve world hunger by extending the hours for room service.

A Palm Beacher's idea of bucking the system is to use paper napkins on picnics."

"What do they do for entertainment?"

"Drink, mainly. In Palm Beach a sexual deviant is someone who prefers women to martinis. You can't blame them, though. If you try to face Palm Beach Society fully conscious, you fall asleep."

"It sounds like hell."

"Not quite. You can enter hell on merit; in Palm Beach you have to know somebody to get in."

"I want you to write a response to this Wiggins fellow. Attack Palm Beach just as he attacked Iowa. You know, fight fire with fire."

"That's petty, chief. I don't think we should descend to his level. Besides, put yourself in Wiggins' shoes. Suppose you were a Palm Beach columnist. Suppose you were bored."

"You're repeating yourself, Don, but I guess you're right. We'll let it pass. No Palm Beach jokes. By the way, do you know how to tell when a Palm Beach marriage is on the rocks?"

"No. How?"

"The couple stops exchanging Christmas cards."

IOWA GO BRA – JOKES THAT LIFT AND ELEVATE

Now let us proceed with a new kind of joke specifically tailored to boost, not roast. For a joke to work there must be an element of truth to build on. And the happy truth is that Iowans are so chock full of down home virtues that our only recourse is to focus on those virtues and to – well embroider a bit.

To an Iowan these observations may not always come off as funny because the truths expressed strike them as commonplace. For example, Iowa youngsters learn party manners before their first birthday party.

"Do not reach for the biggest piece of cake," they are cautioned by their mothers. "Do not ask for seconds until everyone has been served and then you wait to be asked if you want more."

Iowans take such instruction to heart. Party hosts know to use a protractor to slice cake in perfectly even slices. Otherwise NOBODY ever takes that biggest piece of cake.

Exasperated party moms have been known to shriek, "It's just a piece of cake, for pity's sake. Somebody take it before you drive the dog crazy and then we can play Twister."

All that the party goers hear is "Twister!" and everybody heads for the basement and the dog gets that big piece of cake.

So what you are about to read might now and again make you laugh if you are an Iowan, or if you know an Iowan. What's truly funny about Iowans is that they are serenely unaware of their innate adorability. To spend time with Iowans is to feel like you've collected $200 for not passing Go.

What I'm telling you about Iowa in the guise of jokes and anecdotes will come out in dribs and drabs to give you the whole picture, but just consider this: Le Mars Iowa is the home of Blue Bunny Premium Homemade Vanilla Ice Cream and the annual Le Mars Ice Cream Days that draws 100,000 people every June. I think that tells you something.

So here they come, still more of the only positive stereotyping jokes aimed at an entire unsuspecting state population.

Iowa has the quietest public libraries in the nation, but at a cost.

Q: At a cost? What cost?
A: Last year 17 Iowans were hushed to death in public libraries.

Iowa beauty contestants are so genuinely gracious that each year there is one Miss Iowa and 19 girls tied for Miss Congeniality.

It's hard to get a handle on just how good Iowans are until you realize that no Iowan has ever poured grease down the sink or clogged the disposal with artichoke leaves.

Iowans keep their houses so neat that they aren't familiar with the concept of spring cleaning. Mothers-in-law don't even bother with surprise visits.

When an Iowan gal tells you she can't go out with you because she has to starch and iron her mops, she means that she has to starch and iron her mops.

Iowans are born knowing how to fold a fitted sheet.

Iowans are super respectful. When eating off their Elvis Presley Memorial Dinner Plate, they do not consider it amusing to leave peas over Elvis' eyes

Iowan teens are not above youthful hijinks. Some do go in for cow tipping. Fifteen percent is customary, 20 percent for extraordinary service.

Iowans try not to be judgmental but if they see you in the HOV lane without passengers they *will* wonder how your mother raised you.

Iowans have a crisis of conscience at red lights at 2 a.m. on an empty street when no cops are around. They wait for the light to change, but they're asking themselves, "Why am I out at 2 o'clock in the morning?"

Iowans not only watch their slang, they won't say cow pie with a mouthful. Not because they avoid barnyard terminology, but because they know it's not polite to talk with your mouth full.

Time for a fudge break.

OH, FUDGE!

There, I said it. The F-word. Fudge. People used to say "Oh, fudge" all the time, in moments of vexation, like when you had the beaters half way out the mixing bowls and bumped the whip button for that panoramic decorative effect you weren't really looking for.

I miss fudge. I miss "Oh, my stars and garters," "Land sakes alive", "For crying out loud," and "Oh, my sweet Aunt Fanny," said with feeling. I miss my dad saying, "Good grief!" and "Good gravy!" and "Hey, you kids pipe down in there!"

Remember the Snuffy Smith comic and how "Land o' Goshen" served as an expletive, yet seemed to have the Sunday school stamp of approval on it? It's a fine fudge substitute.

Years ago, I went on a one man crusade to bring back manly slang full of soul satisfying fricatives, and hard consonants you can say through clenched teeth. I gave my crusade a catchy name with a nifty acronym:

F.U.D.G.E.

Which stands for Folks United to Discourage Gutter Expletives.

FUDGE never went anywhere because the few people to buy F.U.D.G.E. tee-shirts complained that wearing them made them hungry.

But for now, I am declaring all Iowans honorary F.U.D.G.E. members. So now, in the immortal words of Mayor Shinn, in "The Music Man", **"Watch your phraseology!"**

The following slang expressions are FUDGE-approved for parlor use in the company of Iowans, **Nebraskans, South** and **North Carolinians, Georgians, Arkansans, Oklahomans, Minnesotans, Mississipians, Lousianans, Alabamans** and **Canadians.**

- Sufferin' succotash!
- Ratzen-fratz!
- By thunder!
- Oh, my sweet Aunt Fanny!
- Ye gads!
- Cheese and rice got all muddy!
- Godfrey Daniel!
- Well, I'll be dipped!
- Rats!
- Sassasfras!
- Well, comb my hair and call me shorty!
- Criminey!
- Tough toenails!
- Mother of Pearl!
- So help me, Hannah!
- Great Scott!
- Son of a sea cook!
- Jumping Jehoshaphat!
- Leapin' lizards!
- Good gravy!
- John Jacob Jingle Heimer Smith!
- Kiss my foot!

FUDGE nominations always welcome at: www.iowanice. com

YES, WE PROFILE IOWANS, AND YOU PROBABLY ARE AN IOWAN, YOU LUCKY DOG, IF…

- You dot your i's and cross your t's, mind your p's and q's, and your manners.
- You never pick at it, and it gets well.
- You don't go much for smutty talk in mixed company and anyone can make you blush by merely saying "Frederick's of Hollywood under the mattress."
- A boy asks you out and you almost automatically say "yes" because you assume it's to the Dairy Queen. Second dates tend to be for ice cream at your house with your mom serving up dishes of Blue Bunny so she can report to your dad.
- You know you really like the girl and show her you mean business on that Dairy Queen date by ordering the Brownie Delight piled high with whipped cream and fudge topping, two spoons.
- You play peek-a-hello because you don't want to scare the baby.
- The meanest thing you've ever said to another Iowan is, "I hope you inherit a pumpkin patch and they call off Halloween."

IOWA KIDS

Iowan kids save M&Ms for later. They still have Halloween candy tucked in the freezer at Easter. Iowan dads do not cherry pick the good stuff from the trick or treat haul. Taking out all the Hershey's and Snickers can get you hauled in for family counseling.

And when kids do "trick" by soaping your windows, they also rinse and finish with a squeegee.

Iowa kids not only put the cap back on the toothpaste, they wipe the bristle foam flecks off the mirror with Windex and a paper towel.

When an Iowa mom packs a school lunch, she finds a thank you note in the lunch box for yesterday's, along with a review:

"The diagonal sandwich cut was geometric perfection and the egg salad had that perfect balance of mayo and mustard with chopped olives that only the best moms can achieve. The half a Ho-Ho nestled against the half Twinkie oozing their creamy goodness made me go back and say a second grace, this time with feeling. I ❤ you, Mom. Randy."

Sure, Iowa kids squabble in the back seat – nobody said they're perfect – but they bicker quietly, by passing notes.

Iowa teenagers are truthful with their parents, but considerate, parceling out information on a need-to-know basis, with a fine regard for what will upset them.

Iowa kids can time the school bus' arrival with split second accuracy, but get to the stop five minutes early just to keep their mothers' nerves unfrazzled.

Iowa kids can spot a tense parental back from across the room and be there with a magic fingers neck and shoulder rub. Adult Iowans have incredible will power acquired as kids by sucking their Tootsie Pops all the way down to the soft chocolate center without biting through the hard candy shell.

More Truthhoods

Patience? Iowans are as patient as a sink full of dirty dishes.

Even Iowan rednecks have class. They build prim white picket fences with planters around their junked cars.

Iowan fishermen deliberately backlash their casts just for the relaxation of unsnarling the mess.

Iowan home makers believe the Perma-Prest label on shirts and pants, but they iron anyway. Just for good measure.

An Iowan, Enos Archer of Ames, was the nation's top retail clothing salesman, remarkable, in that he sold men's underwear, specializing in one brand. He was Fruit of the Loom's top *drawer* salesman.

Hysterical footnote: A Duck Walk, **Ohio** salesman, Emile Frotage, specialized in womens' panties, pulling down 30,000 a year. He was unhappy in his work, and when his wife said, "Emile, the trouble with you is that you don't take time to smell the roses," he replied, "Don't go there."

Iowan girls are not prone to kiss on the first date. In fact, their parents teach them not to remain pretty much vertical until after marriage.

Even when properly and primly perpendicular to the ground, Iowa gals can still be smoking hot. Young men too thick to sense when a kiss would be appropriate have been slow-danced into a quivering mound of highly cooperative testosterone.

Iowans learn to swim as well anyone else, but they make lousy lifeguards because they refuse to go into the water until an hour after eating.

Last year eleven Jay Walkers were listed in Iowa phone books, but not one jay walker listed in court records.

Iowans ticketed for traffic infractions not only elect to take traffic school to avoid points, but strive to graduate *summa cum laude*. Kids have bike bumper stickers bragging "My mom made traffic school honor roll."

IOWA VS. MISSOURI

A vacationing blonde Iowa State Trooper was giving her Mustang convertible some Interstate exercise when she was pulled over by a male counterpart from her neighboring state.

Before flashing her badge and hoping for some professional courtesy, she decided to have a little fun with the state cop, so batting her eyes like mad, she asked him:

"Oh, officer, did you want to ask me to the Trooper's ball?"

"Lady," he snapped, "I'll have you know that Missouri state troopers don't have balls."

"Oh, you poor dears," she said.

The Missourian spent an entire five seconds mute behind his Ray-Bans, reflecting on what he had just said, then murmured, "Oh, my sweet lord," and went elsewhere.

JOKES RUB IOWA
TRANSPLANT THE RIGHT WAY

Judging by mail response to my gentle observations on the Hawkeye State, Iowans are roughly divided between fans who want more news from Iowa, and detractors who say I'm a smart alec who needs an ounce of my flesh removed from a place where I would miss it most.

My goal is to get all Iowans on board with the likes of Terry Eilbert of Jupiter, FL, who writes:

"My husband and I moved here from Iowa 10 years ago, and since then have eagerly anticipated and enjoyed your Iowan columns. At various times you have described some Iowans so well that we were sure you *must* know these people personally as we do.

"In one article your descriptions reminded me of my father-in-law. Honestly, he never turned his Rubik's cube because he thought the colors looked nice just the way it came!"

Terry then goes on to call my attention to an enclosed clipping from *The Jefferson Herald* reporting on a local fair's "cow patty contest" reported as follows:

"According to contest chairman Jack Fineseth, the game involves releasing a steer into a pasture west of the post office.

The field will be divided into 2 feet by 2 feet numbered squares. The owner of the square upon which the steer deposits his "patty" will win $250."

In that column I thanked Terry for her kind words and the news item from Jefferson. Cow patty Lotto, I predicted, would evolve into a state lottery with scratch and sniff tickets. If it smells mighty unlike a rose, you could be a big winner.

As for the Eilberts' plea for me to dip into my growing file of Iowa lore, I was happy to oblige:

Iowans are so good about answering the phone after the first ring that it's hard for them to watch cop shows with phones constantly ringing in the background. If nobody picks up the phone, they break out in hives.

I was joshing when I originally reported that Iowans tend to excitability about small joys and cry out "That's me!" when getting mail addressed to occupant. But the truth is that Iowans are so respectful of the privacy of others that they forward any occupant mail meant for a former tenant.

Iowan tennis players call themselves on foot faults.

Iowans who catch themselves cheating at solitaire send themselves to bed without any supper.

Even Iowan toddlers are brought up scrupulously honest from the cradle and won't tell you "I'm 3 going on 4 unless they are absolutely positive that 4 comes after 3.

If an Iowan asks her friend at city hall to fix a parking ticket, the friend will tear the ticket in two, slap a piece of tape on it and return it, saying, "There, fixed good as new. Now pay the $25 and beat it before I call your mother."

Iowa is the only state with failed gubernatorial candidates still paying off 30-year-old campaign debts, $5 a week.

BLUSHING GROOMS PART I

Nebraska

On their wedding night the eager bride of a **Nebraskan** youth waxed impatient in her diaphanous peignoir while her newly-minted husband spent quite a bit of time on his knees, hands folded in supplication.

"What are you doing?" she asked at length.

"Why darling, I'm praying for guidance," he replied.

"I'll handle the guidance, bub," she said. "You pray for endurance."

Blushing Grooms Part II
South Dakota

A **South Dakotan** bride, same night, same hotel, was puzzled to see her pajama-clad soul mate standing by himself, staring out the window for the greater part of an hour. Clad in diaphanous raiment and cleared for action, she had had quite enough of this chastity business, and gently inquired of her husband what was so all-fired interesting on the other side of that window?

Turning to her and smiling sweetly, he said:

"Mother told me that tonight would be the most beautiful night of my life, and I don't want to miss a single minute of it."

Three minutes later the South Dakota bride was in the lounge knocking back Stingers with the Nebraska bride and re-thinking the whole situation

Your state ain't doodley-squat

Hysterical note: I don't know if my original salvo of Iowa jokes triggered some of the interstate pot-shotting of the next few years, but I didn't have to be asked twice to stoke the fires when kindly readers sent them my way. Here's some half-witti-cisms constituting the cream of the dregs of my mail bag.

For a brief period radio DJs from Iowa and Minnesota were going at it hammer and scythe. Unlike my attempts at humor, the idea was to denigrate, not compliment. I don't approve of mean Iowan jokes and I barely tolerate them about other states, and when *I* make a putdown joke, I feel dirty for days.

Tit

Q: Why don't **Minnesotans** drink more Kool-Aid?
A: Because they can't figure out how to get two quarts of water in one of those little envelopes.

Tat

Q: Why do football fields in Iowa have artificial turf?
A: To discourage the cheerleaders from grazing.

OK, you can see that these "jokes" are heavy-handed insults, so we continue with scant relish. Scant relish, by the way is what you get on your hot dog at the **Illinois** State Fair.

Tit

Q: What is the difference between **Minnesota** and yogurt?
A: Yogurt has culture.

Tat

Q: What do you call two dirty Teddy Bears and a tractor that won't start?
A: The Iowa State Fair.

Tit

Q: What is printed on the bottom of beer bottles in **Minnesota?**
A: Open other end.

Tat

Not really a **tat** because this gag is a place holder for a **tat**, just as you can't have a shave and a haircut without a two bits. It's practically the law.

Q: What do Iowans do when they can't level a pool table?
A: They knock off the legs and play on the ground.

ABE GETS OFF A ZINGER

It was Abe Lincoln, ironically enough, who started the Jokes Between the States when the felled president was asked by a frantic Secret Serviceman, "Lordy, lordy, Mr. President? Who has shot you so cruelly?"

"Five hundred Mississippi sharpshooters," Abe said, quickly adding, "just joshing."

Upbeat Vermont Joke, the Kind I Like

Finishing a job, a surveying crew foreman approached a farmer repairing a fence to deliver what he was afraid would be disturbing news.

"Sir, we've had to correct the state line with the help of one of those geo-synchronous satellites up there, and it turns out the line was way off. You don't live in Vermont. As of right now, you and your farm are in New Hampshire."

An uncomfortable silence ensued as the farmer reflected on what it all meant.

"Well, sir," resumed the foreman, "we were wondering how you feel about living in New Hampshire now?"

The farmer nodded gravely and said: "Thank goodness. I don't think I could have made it through another Vermont winter."

Maine, the strict economies state

A factory manager scouting for a new site in Maine was being squired around town by the mayor and a spray of lesser dignitaries when he noticed a raggedy fellow getting rude treatment from the group.

Twice they passed by the man, muttering at him under their breaths and even jostling him off the sidewalk. The out-of-towner wondered what kind of outrage this seemingly harmless soul could have committed to deserve such abuse.

"Say, your honor," he whispered to the mayor, "what's the story on that fellow everybody seems so down on?"

"Oh, him! We don't talk about him. Just ignore him."

"That bad?" pressed the factory manager.

"Well, if you must know," the mayor exhaled, "some years ago, he *dipped into his capital!*"

Belittling Rhode Island Joke

Q: Why did they close the Providence Zoo?
A: The clam died.

Deep in the boondocks of Texas

Remember that Vermont survey crew? This time they're in Texas at the end of a bitter January Wednesday when walking out of the woods to their truck, they hear church music.

"Hey, must be a prayer meeting," says one of the surveyors. "Can't be a half mile. Let's go." The guys had been passing a bottle to ward off the cold, and were in a convivial mood when they took seats in the back pew, grabbed hymnals and added their lusty voices to the singing.

Smiling in welcome, the preacher added a few more hymns for the newcomers' benefit, and truly joyful voices of congregation and surveyors united in melodious praise to the heavens. At last, the preacher closed his hymnal, intoning, "And now, let us pray."

"Aw, hell no!" cried out the crew chief, jumping up in protest. "Let's *sang* some more!"

More interstate sniping

Q: What do you call a Long Island Sound garbage scow adrift in the fog?
A: New Jersey

Cold Shoulder

Alaska just might be the most boring state when you consider that after the Iditarod, the state's most exciting event is the annual Spot-welding and Lichen Festival.

Runner up boring state is...

North Dakota. The state disease is cabin fever. By the spring thaw everybody in the state is running around the house on all fours. When a North Dakotan answers the door, he props his forearms on your shoulders and laps your face.

Minnesotans, dependably easy-going, can be a bit cranky in the early spring – their winter pelts are still shedding.

Washington State – Knee-deep when wet

Wet? I'll say. The only difference between west **Washington State** and a cranberry bog is that once a year they drain the cranberry bog (from the internet).

Kumbaya-fornia

This is a retread of an old California Bay Area joke. Suck it up and read it. Anyway, Sponge Bob, deceased, was given a furlough from heaven to go to Fisherman's Wharf for seafood and dancing, and to see his old friend, Sam Clam whose restaurant featured a BeeGees sound-alike group. Sponge Bob had such a good time drinking and dancing that he forgot his harp.

"Where's your harp?" asked St. Peter.

"Oh, no!" he gasped. "I left my harp in Sam Clam's Disco!"

Nevada: a 1951 Reader's Digest Knee-slapper

A motorist, noticing thunderheads building up over Death Valley, remarked to the old timer pumping his gas in a little store at the edge of nowhere, "Looks like rain headed this way."

"Hope so," replied the elderly gent. "Not for me so much, but the young ones. I've seen rain."

Constructive criticism for Wisconsin

I'm sorry, but The Dairy State doesn't do this marvelous state enough credit. Wisconsin is the *cheese* state, and that cannot be stressed enough. The state motto should be, and let's carve this in parmesan:

There is no such thing as cheesy enough!

Have you ever had macaroni that was too cheesy or with a chewy cheesy crust that overwhelmed the pasta? No! Neither can pizza be too cheesy. How about a bowl of French onion soup that you had to send back to the kitchen because there was more chewy cheese crust than onion?

Here's your Wisconsin license plate: *There is no such thing as cheesy enough*! That ought to be on every license plate in **Wisconsin**. If Wisconsin is looking for a cheese czar, I'm their man.

Bonus note: How to make a box of macaroni and cheese edible: Grate a block of extra-sharp cheddar cheese until you have a pile the size of a termite mound and add it to that pathetic orange powder they give you in the box. Now you've got something.

According to my Iowa mail:

- Iowa cats come when called.
- Iowa cats eat dry dog food in a spirit of gratitude.
- Iowa cats don't have hairballs. In fact, when they get hair on their tongues, they sensibly spit it out.
- When guests overstay, Iowa cats sleep on their faces.
- Iowan dogs refuse food from the table.
- Iowan dogs won't accept a chew toy if they don't know where it's been.
- True, Iowa dogs, like other dogs, drink from the toilet, but they remember to put the seat down
- Iowans still say "Last one in is a rotten egg" and "Oh, fudge!"
- Iowans go very light on profanity unless you count "Oh, my sweet Aunt Fanny!"
- Iowan farmers breed corn to grow as high as an elephant's eye so they can see when it's time to shoo the elephants. Oklahoma stole credit for the idea by sneaking the line into their song.
- Tough Iowans have "Born to raise crops" tattooed on their shoulders.
- Iowa pilots get bumper stickers that say, "I'm high on ethanol." The hard part is attaching bumpers to their airplanes.

Vintage Arkansas Moonshining Story

A Floridian driving through the Ozarks goes into a country store to pay for his gas and glances at some squirrel rifle toting locals swapping a jug around.

"Here, have a swig," offers one of the imbibers congenially.

"No thanks, I'm driving," replies the motorist.

"I said drink!" growls the mountaineer, shoving the jug up to the traveler's mouth and the rifle into his gut. The flatlander manages two swallows before gagging and spluttering.

"Why that's awful!" exclaims the Floridian. "How can you drink that stuff?"

"Ain't it, though?" grins the Arkansan, handing the stranger the rifle. "Now hold the gun on me and I'll swaller."

Iowa mouthwash: a bar of Octagon soap, sovereign for potty mouth. If condition persists, consider woodshed counseling.

High school students don't smoke in school. If you see smoke coming out of the boys room, the school is on fire."

A few Iowans join nudist colonies, but they're modest about it. They wear Groucho nose glasses.

In Iowa there is a petition drive to raise the speed limit to 75. Also the drinking age.

In Iowa irregular verbs are heavily discounted.

Iowa reality shows canceled after one episode:

Iowa's Most Wanted: Slow motion re-enactment of a Davenport toilet papering.

Lockup Iowa Style: a state pen prisoner swaps his fruit cup for pudding from a prisoner who wasn't looking, and agrees in reparation to surrender his next three Jell-Os.

Are You Going to Eat That? The fun begins when a pushy New Yorker sits down uninvited next to restaurant patrons, prods the diner's food with his fork, asking," Are you going to eat that?"

Extra! Extra!..Forget it!

In many cities the newspaper is accused of sensationalizing the news. In Iowa it is necessary, witness these recent headlines:

WINTHROP- Caffeine-crazed teenager runs amber light

DEFIANCE- Muffin tin shortage looms

IMOGENE- Pay phones – where the heck did they all go?

CEDAR RAPIDS- Man smuggles popcorn into theater with puffy-sleeved pirate shirt – busted by alert usher who spots wrist drawstrings

THE MICHIGAN AND
DAKOTA STOMP

I'm still annoyed at the **Michigan** woman who jumped on South Florida in the *Detroit Free Press* a few days ago (Author update – it was years and years ago). So I'll just do the logical thing here and malign **North Dakota** and **Montana** after I settle Michigan's hash.

A thin logic to be sure; not the kind of logic you want to skate out on and jump up and down on, but a logic sufficient for my purposes. For one thing, I don't know anything about Michigan except that wolverines eat your paper before you can get to it in the morning and that the state is the supplier of Mackinaw Island fudge; which can be melted and poured over Blue Bunny ice cream.

North Dakota is a much easier target it already being the laughinggoat (like scapegoat, only funnier) of the 300 million Americans who don't live there. North Dakota asked for it by announcing an image overhaul.

North Dakota jokes are now the rage, reports William E. Schmidt of the New York Times:

Q: What is the official tree of North Dakota?
A : The telephone pole.

Only in North Dakota, the story goes, can you find a sign that says "Drive Carefully, No Hospital for 350 miles."

According to the *Times* piece, Mike Dalton, a Great Falls, MT, disc jockey published an entire joke book about the other Vacant State and sold 25,000 copies through radio station KQDI with profits earmarked for charity. Curious and passing strange that Montana would be going after North Dakota when Montana is North Dakota with wrinkles. Maybe colder. I've been to Montana in the winter and it wasn't long before I discovered why nobody smiles at 20 below: you scream when your lips split.

Upgrading North Dakota's Image

Then came director of tourism Mike Foster with a $1.3 million promotions budget to promote tourism. With bean counters figuring that one busload of tourists drops more than $2,000 a day, it was calculated that the image facelift would pay dividends in short order.

After months of brainstorming, a simple punctuation mark was all the boosters could come up with. It actually looked good on a billboard:

North Dakota!

Why not? If Rogers and Hammerstein could take a musical called "Oklahoma" and punch it up by changing the name to "Oklahoma!", why wouldn't it work to add the exclamation mark to North Dakota!?

Actually, it did work. Motorists driving through North Dakota! Reduced their average speed from 105 mph to 70.

Nobody stopped and speeding violations revenues fell from $397 million annually to zero. And that was about that. "North Dakota: It's Nothing like New Jersey" never got much traction, nor were most folks able to make the connection between North Dakota and the **I ♥ Open Pit Lignite Mining** bumper stickers. The jury is still out on the revamped state slogan:

North Dakota! The reasonably rectangular state

OK, that commentary was from a 1982 column, and I want to make amends with North Dakota by saying that I'm a big fan of that state's Ed Schultz, the Paul Bunyonesque radio and TV personality who personally stomped all the mountains out of North Dakota so people could tell it from Montana.

NICE SLOGAN, BUT WILL
IT FIT ON A LICENSE PLATE?

About the time I was becoming a full-fledged fan of Iowa, a transplanted Iowan egged me on with a hometown clipping about Iowa's search for a snappy slogan, something to stop travelers from thinking of Iowa as the Drive-Through State.

Me to Iowa's Rescue

Iowa tourism is in crisis (I wrote) and I must fly
to her with succor. There's a succorer born every minute.

Hawkeyes don't have a catchy slogan that will fit on a license plate, and instead of coming up with a slogan with some pizzazz, the forces of insipidity within the Iowa Department of Transportation are bent on issuing black and white plates with no message.

According to an editorial in the *Grinnell Herald-Register* (courtesy of Darrell and Brenda Ferneau of Okeechobee, FL), Iowa is one of two states out of 50 that does not have a a motto or catch-phrase. California is the other.

(California is easy: The Keratosis State or The Shared Experience State, or even The More Moonbeam than Sunshine State. Florida has a lock on The Sunshine State.)

Iowa is a bit more of a challenge.

And yet a challenge that must be met. As the *Herald-Register* so ably expresses it: "We have to work harder to make sure that travelers think twice before deciding that traveling in Iowa is only to be endured while passing through east, west, north or south to get to someplace else."

While her neighbors have capitalized on the sloganeering mania, Iowa has seen fit to remain modest and unassuming.

Q: How unassuming?
A: Iowans will assume a 4.5 percent 30 year mortgage if the bank throws in a toaster.

Q: By the way, how can you spot the Iowan nudists at a national sun bathers convention?
A: Tattoos: Look for the Good Housekeeping Seal of Approval above the navel.

A few motto/slogans have been tried out for Iowa, but so far, nothing has clicked.

Iowa – the Generic State
Keep Iowa Beige
We're Not in Kansas Anymore, but We Can't Prove It

Sorry, none of the above has pizzazz. To Iowa's credit, no slogan might be better than a slogan that's just embarrassing. Compare:

Georgia – This way to fun
Come see **South Carolina**
Maryland – Capture a Maryland memory
Virginia is for lovers
Feel Free in **South Dakota**

That last sounds great, but feel free to what? Squeeze the peaches in the produce department? You'll get your hand slapped. How about "South Dakota - horizons everywhere you look"?

Florida came to its senses by dropping the long standing "Keep Florida Green" motto which visitors understandably interpreted as "Let's Fleece Tourists". Our incumbent slogan, The Sunshine State may be modified to:

"Florida, the Dermatologist on Every Corner State"

Hands down, the best state slogan is the state put on the map by flying houses and monkeys.

Kansas, the Land of Ah's

Iowa alert – this just in: Des Moines attorney David Belin has a slogan under consideration:

Iowa – Quality and Productivity

That'll go over like seersucker overalls. Let's end this right now with my suggestion for Iowa as a state where you might want to sink roots.

A nice place to visit, but you wouldn't want to leave here!

Nebraska's problematic shape

I could say that I've teased Nebraska because everybody teases Nebraska. Even Iowans. The problem, I would suggest, is that Nebraska has an odd shape. Somebody dropped the corner of Colorado right on Nebraska, disfiguring it beyond dignity. We should ease up.

Someday.

I even teased Nebraska a little on one of the occasions I was joshing Iowa about being such perky paragons of citizenry perfection. I might have called Nebraska dull. Nebraska got wind of the jibe and teased back. Indeed, Jeff Jordan, columnist for the *Omaha Sunday World-Herald* came at me like a steamed shoat (not to be confused with an enraged sow).

Jordan knows his way around a gerund clause and his observations on Florida stung like the dickens. They were also pretty funny:

"Such is the calumny that comes from alligator country – the Bemused Triangle that extends in swampy misery from turgid Tallahassee to jaded Jacksonville to mirthless Miami – where citrus freezes in Frostproof, FL, condos topple into the storm surge, and Disney World rises as a symbol of Sun Belt sunstroke...

Hang in there, Jordan is just getting warmed up:

"Where sophistication means sucking your peanuts out of a Perrier bottle, where pastrami grits are found on the gourmet shelf, where Lotharios stroll the receding beaches in garters, black ankle socks, brown wingtip shoes and Madras shorts.

"Surely, the fellow from the Corps of Engineers was right when he said, 'If it wasn't for the drainage, Florida would simply be a hindrance to navigation.'

"Well, I don't know about you fellow Huskers, but by gum, I think we ought to flat refuse to go to the Orange Bowl again next year."

Jordan writes fancy and funny at the same time. He talks that way too. The story goes that while visiting Boston some years ago, Jordan made grammatical history when he asked a bell captain "Where can I go to get scrod?" and the bell captain declared in awe, "Man and boy I've lived in Boston and to my knowledge you are the first person ever to employ the pluperfect ablative case of that verb!"

My only beef with Jordan is that he gave Florida short shrift. He slighted us by not slamming us enough. I didn't feel the love.

Here's some more Tru Florida Facks from a native:

Coastal Florida is so humid on summer nights that fish get confused and have to be squeegeed back into the ocean the next morning.

The sun is brutal. South Florida resident and Pulitzer Prize essayist Dave Barry has personally witnessed flamingos bursting into flames while circling the Hialeah Race Track.

This past summer a red-haired Delaware resident visiting New Smyrna Beach on a cloudless day slapped on five brands of 100 SPF solar screen, two layers of zinc oxide applied with a spackle knife, and then huddled under a beach umbrella all day. When life guards found him at 5 p.m. he had frozen to death.

In a desperate attempt to bolster Florida's farm economy, the Orville Redenbacher's labs were asked to develop a Florida brand of gourmet popping sandspurs. It didn't work. They tried crossing sandspurs with peanuts and came up with peanut butter that really sticks to the roof of your mouth.

Q: Why don't vampires vacation in Florida?
A: The mosquitoes make them take a number and wait.

Praise for Nebraska

In 2009 Nebraska surpassed Iowa for the first time in pork productivity with hogs taken to market outweighing Iowa hogs by an average of 30 lbs. Their secret: Swill Helper.

By an amazing coincidence, Husker linemen for the first time tipped the scales 30 lbs. heavier than their University of Iowa counterparts the same year. Their training table secret?... Uh, I forget.

Joisy Crude vs. Hawkeye Shrewd

Entering her dorm room for the first time, an Iowan co-ed is about to introduce herself to her New Jersey roomie when the Jersey girl roars:

"Close that damn door, you ninny! Were you raised in a barn?"

The Iowa lass flings herself onto her bed sobbing as if heart to burst.

Taken aback, the Jersey co-ed says, "My gawd, I didn't mean to upset you."

"Oh, it's nothing," sniffs the Iowan, lifting her head with a wan smile. "It's just that I *was* raised in a barn and every time I hear an ass bray I get homesick."

ARE IOWANS MISSING THE SNEAKY GENE?

In 1986 there was a story about Iowan employees of two defense contractors selling secrets. Apparently, there was nothing to it because charges were never placed. I could have told investigators that Iowans are too honest to be spies.

Q: Why are Iowan applications to the C.I.A. routinely rejected?
A: Because when declaring that they would lie for their country, they break out in a cold sweat, their noses grow, and their tongues turn black.

In WWII landlocked Iowan draft boards didn't quite know what to make of the "Loose lips sink ships" posters that were appearing everywhere. To play it safe they flunked every draftee with a lip wobble exceeding seven millimeters.

Iowan P.O.W. interrogators, curiously enough, got the quickest results by using a Gestapo line on German prisoners: "We have ways of making you talk." And they did have ways: They asked pretty please with sugar on it, and if that didn't work, they broke out the "Whoopee John Wilfahrt" polka records and played them without mercy.

MORE STATE SLANDER

Q: What was the rumor that brought the economy of Oregon to the brink of collapse and threw the entire state into mourning?
A: That Juan Valdez was dead.

Q: How do you throw the entire staff of a Portland coffee shop into confusion during morning rush hour?
A: Ask for a cup of coffee, black.

See, that's how it starts. A love tap escalating to a slap, then a noogie, a shoulder punch that raises a "frog", then the little guy wets his finger and sticks it into the big guy's ear and finally somebody's squealing from the outrage of a pink belly while from the front seat we hear:

"That's it, I'm stopping the car and the both of you are really going to get it!"

These sibling state insult fests have to stop. After they run their course, natch, and I'm here to help with that. For my part, I have introduced the compliment joke, a lone Floridian buttering up Iowans whom I offer up as the model citizens we all would be had we listened to our mothers. This I demonstrate by describing the little quirks and endearing ways of Iowans that make us just want to scoop them up and blow rude spit bubbles on their sweet little tummies.

You want Iowa Niceness? Here's your Iowa Niceness:

Iowa Golfers

Q: The Iowan golfer has just sliced into the woods. Why is he smiling?
A: He's thinking, "Easter Egg hunt!"

Q: Ask an Iowan golfer, which would you rather do, shoot your best round ever, or find nine like-new Titelist DTs?
A: Come back later. He's still deciding.

Q: An Iowa golfer just hit a low, raking worm-burner into the lake, he turns to his pals, grinning, and they're slapping high fives. Why?
A: Seven skips.

Don't Make Me Stop This Narrative

See, if you can't say something nice – be from **Connecticut** or **Rhode Island**. A few years ago both states were swapping insults. Steve and Linda Huggins, Jupiter, FL residents, sent two sample jokes.

Q: Why does Harford have a law against educating dogs? - this is an actual law – you can look it up. The answer, of course, is a wild guess.
A: Nobody likes an elitist dog.

Q: How did Connecticut and Rhode Island ever agree to be the only two states not to ratify the Eighteenth Amendment establishing Prohibition?
A: They drank to it.

When Indiana Woos Iowa

Iowa girls wouldn't hurt a boy's feelings for anything, but when an Indiana lad is showing signs of being full to the eyebrows of himself, he can depend upon her to restore his perspective.

Indiana BMOC: "Baby, it's getting late. Isn't it about time you went into your bedroom and slipped into something more comfortable?"

Iowa girl: "Yeah, a coma."

Iowans Relish the Moment

Life rains little blessings on us every day, but it takes an Iowan to stop and smell the Juicy Fruit wrappers.

When an Iowan sees a waxed floor he kicks off his shoes and slides in his socks.

Iowan bus riders like to be the one who leans over the curb and says "Here comes the bus!" This has resulted in mass topplings, and great loss of Life Savers going down the wrong pipe.

Iowans, generally a pretty low key bunch, can work up exceptional enthusiasm. It's kind of a rule that when you drive up beside another car that is a clone of your own, the first one to set their car in park, jump out of the car, point to the other car and cry "Twins!" is owed a small cone at the next DQ. The ritual is celebrated with great merriment and fist bumps.

I salute Iowans and seek to emulate them in savoring life's little pleasures. Iowans understand that when their favorite song comes on the car radio and finishes just as they slide into their parking spot, that the universe has just blown them a kiss.

Iowans delight in butter cookie nibbling contest to see who can eat away cookie and leave the slimmest ring in the middle? First one to break the ring is a rotten egg!

A genuine pleasure you can enjoy again and again is a dog that is an eager eater. When Iowans have such a dog they like to have company over so they can say: "You think your dog can go to town on a bowl of Gravy Train? Watch this!"

Iowans love recommending books to friends and experience joy verging on rapture when the friend apologizes for yawning in their faces by saying, "Sorry, that book you gave me was so good, I stayed up half the night reading it."

A cheap thrill for an Iowan is having the drop of fudge congeal on the first try when dropped into water. She is even more thrilled when the damn stuff never does harden because at that moment she can cry out, "Break out the Blue Bunny Vanilla – hot fudge sundaes NOW!"

When it's raining and the sun is shining at the same time, Iowans get a cheap thrill of being the first to say, "Check it out, the devil is beating his wife." Iowans learned that expression when they were little kids. Did you? You did? Hey, maybe you're part Iowan.

Iowans and folks you can't hardly tell from Iowans...

Learn thrift and planning for the future as kids by saving M&Ms for later.

Find more joy browsing a used book store than big city jet-setters get out of a dash to Paris for dinner.

Exult in thrift store designer clothes finds.

Get an adrenaline rush from living on the edge by digging their toast out with a fork.

Would never hide the last piece from a 1,000-piece jig saw puzzle, then flaunt it in triumphant procession to complete the picture, not if she didn't want bubble gum in her hair.

Try to jump up in the air the instant the elevator drops for extra hang time.

Still like to spin on a piano stool and tuck in their arms for extra rpms.

Lift a 3-year-old up to pull the bell cord for the next bus stop.

Can make a cootie-catcher and turn a 3-year-old whiner into a giggler in 90 seconds.

Are not upset at seeing her dress on another woman at a party – unless her "twin" got a bigger discount; and then there's the "triplet" who shows up in the same dress.

No. 1: "Isn't it darling? I got it 40 percent off at Furchgot's."

No. 2: "I waited 'til Wednesday for an extra 15 percent off."

No. 3: "Mine fell off a truck and was run over three times and I got it for free. See? Tread marks!"

No Stress marks on Iowa and Nebraska

The Associated Press reported that the least stressful place to live in the United States are Iowa and Nebraska.

How unstressful is Hawkeye and Husker life?

According to findings reported by the Family Resources Laboratory at the University of New Hampshire, both states ranked extremely low in personal and family misfortunes such as personal bankruptcy with 16 points each. By contrast, **Nevada** was the most stressful state with 104, and Alaska a distant second with 87.

Get on with it. Bring on the jokes. How unstressed is Iowa?

Well, if you really must know...

We must, we must!

Because Iowans and Nebraskans gets so little stress to cope with, the least little thing can overload their nervous systems and pack them off to the laughing academy.

Public health officials have taken precautions: Iowa and Nebraska share a Tangled Coat Hanger Hotline.

Iowans and Nebraskans have no blood pressure at all. Doctors consult tide tables.

In the Midwest in general, where all bread basket states boasted low stress levels, the sole Rolaids salesman for 100,000 square miles knows how to spell relief. He's on it.

Suicides are all but unknown although, a Nebraskan, despondent after getting soap-on-a-rope for Christmas, ate an oyster in a month without an R.

Researchers say some stress is good. That's why the dangerously under-stressed get the toy where you try to tilt the BBs into the clown's eyes. Iowan and Nebraskan MENSA members get an all white Rubik's Cube with numbers representing colors.

Stress-starved school kids beg for pop quizzes that count double on their grades.

You can't just go into a department store in either state and ask for a nap rug. You must specify type of nap rug - child, adult, group, or stadium.

Midwesterners as a general rule are such good sleepers that they sleep walk the last five steps to the bed. Iowa and Nebraska are the only states where you can buy pillow cases with racing stripes.

AN ACTUAL TELLING JOKE HERE

A Nebraskan goes to the shrink and says, "Doc, my job is so high-stress I gotta have a tranquilizer."

"I can't do that," replies the psychiatrist. "You're the switch-man on the old Topeka line south of town and there hasn't been a train through there in 15 years. What's stressful about that?"

"The suspense is killing me."

A second telling joke

On a cold day a rural Nebraskan dozes off with his feet too close to the fire. His brogan smolders, then bursts into flame.

"Hey, Pa," drawl his son (OK, so this is really a **hillbilly** joke), "your foot's on fire."

"Be specific boy, which one?"

Three in a row

A laconic Iowan returns his basset hound in a wheelbarrow to the pet store. The store owner watches with mild interest as the owner spills the inert beast onto the floor. The animal spreads on the tile like a throw rug, but doesn't complain. Next, his owner grabs two hands full of loose skin on either end and drags the un-protesting beast to the cash register where the animal capsizes and proceeds to snore.

"I want you to take him back and return my money," the Iowan demands.

"What for? He appears to be alive and if he's sick we can't guarantee health."

"Sick isn't the problem. This one's too high strung."

YOU MIGHT BE AN IOWAN IF…

You work in an office where every Friday is Someone I Love More than Life Itself Gave Me This Tie Day

Aug. 17 is Knock off at Noon and Sort Socks Day. Just try reaching an Iowan at work after lunch.

You practice crawling to a phone in case some day you have to.

You smuggle raisins and semi-sweet chocolate morsels into the movie and make Raisenettes in your mouth.

You have prehensile toes. Iowans, according to experts who study this sort of thing, have viciously prehensile toes that can pinch like the dickens. Call an Iowan at random and ask what's up, and if he's honest, he'll say "I'm clenching golf balls in my toes and walking around the house on my heels, why?"

If you hear the stadium announcer say that the owner of the Toyota left his lights on.

FREE RANGE ONE-LINERS
HARVESTED FROM WWW.IOWA.COM –
YOU MAY BE AN IOWAN...

If you drill through a foot of ice and sit in front of the hole all day hoping food will swim by.

If someone at a store helps you and they don't work there.

If you measure distance in hours.

If driving is better in winter because the potholes are packed with snow.

You get a wrong number and you end up talking twenty minutes.

Your car insurance carries a higher deductible for hitting a deer.

If you do hit a deer, you have the marinade and the grill.

You design Halloween costumes to fit over a snowsuit.

Your idea of artistic landscaping is a deer statue in front of a blue spruce.

You swear your truck runs better on ethanol.

You already know what's causing the big traffic jam up ahead– 40 cars and trucks waiting to pass a tractor.

Your school bus ride was long enough to start and finish your homework on the way to school.

You put up security lights and never lock anything.

Your body will accept Mountain Dew for transfusion if your blood type isn't handy.

1987 headline: Iowan prosperity shuns ostentation.

I didn't even have to read the *Los Angeles Times* story to pen yet another mash note to my favorite Midwestern state: Iowa.

I readily admit to an obsession with Iowans that borders on stalking. Iowa, I am convinced, is the bedrock of civic virtue, honor, respect for others and hand washing after everything, and lest I forget – the Iowa Caucus. Even as I write this in 2011, I envision Iowans, their leaf blowers at full throttle, patiently blowing the politicians off their lawns.

Now some might say I am preserving a gossamer fantasy by praising folks I only know by reputation and reportage by others. What if I actually get around to visiting Iowa only to learn that here is not the place of community spelldowns, taffy pulls, bake sales, husking bees and volunteer fire department car washes? My devastation would be total.

I would don a shroud and walk slowly (so as not to cause a panic) into my brown study and there remain until somebody baked brownies.

Happily, all that I hear and read about Iowa only reinforces my first impressions.

And now, this just in – a quarter century ago - from the *Los Angeles Times,* reporting that Iowa was excusing itself from any national malaise requiring handouts or Willie Nelson concerts. Indeed, the *Times* reported, Iowa was flourishing and folks didn't like talking about it.

With personal income up 9.7 percent and unemployment bumping along at 4.6 percent (this was 1987 mind you), Iowa Gov. Terry Branstad said:

"Iowans are different from people in California – they are afraid to admit they are making money. They are afraid of what the neighbors may say."

BINGO! I KNEW IOWANS
WERE DIFFERENT! VINDICATION!

There will be a short intermission here while I thumb my suspenders, fog my nails, and polish them on my vest.

That yellowing *Times* article dovetails with my own findings that: Iowans are very particular about their money and their bankers know it. Withdrawals, I noted in the Foreword, are brought in the same knotted hankie that opened the account.

Iowans, while remarkably free of the usual prejudices, find themselves uncomfortable in the presence of anyone known to have dipped into savings. Play dates have been cancelled. Then in dark of night food baskets appear on doorsteps.

Iowans, for all their teeth-gnashing about the "Infernal Revenue", are bears about declaring all their income. Butter and egg money, bingo winnings, holiday cash gifts, tips, yard sale proceeds, babysitting income – it's all there.

Iowan scrupulousness drives IRS clerks nuts. "Here's another Iowan declaring a $7 Water-Pik rebate."

Although many Iowans can afford to fly first class they don't want to be thought to be putting on the dog, so they slip on Groucho nose glasses when the coach passengers board.

At upscale Iowan restaurants valet parking is self-serve.

Prosperous farmers feel sheepish about driving fancy new pickup trucks with all the bells and whistles, so they pretend to shift.

Iowans who have lost confidence in banks nevertheless are prudent – they only hide money in mattresses insured by the FDIC.

Iowa is the only state with case-hardened stainless steel cookie jars sunk in concrete.

Q: Just how safe is money loaned to an Iowan?
A: The Swiss are talking about replacing the Euro with the Iowa I.O.U.

Iowans still do handshake deals. Later on, if they agree to change the terms, they tear up the handshake.

Iowan job jar culture

Almost nobody in the other 49 gets caught up with the honey-do list. The exception is Iowa where husbands gaze forlornly into empty job jars. They nag their wives for more projects.

TEAR ALONG DOTTED LINE

"I'm bored. I have nothing to do. That last job didn't take long enough. Where's the ladder? I think I'll go up and make the roof leak."

If you're an Iowan, chances are...

You're a bear about dumping the toaster crumbs.

The shower curtain goes into the wash with the towels. Some Iowans plan a trip to Florida just to see what mildew looks like.

You fold your laundry still warm out of the dryer because your mother taught you that a basket of clothing left overnight takes a mean wrinkle-set.

You consider ironing and talking on the phone a form of rest and relaxation.

You never forget to change the rice in the salt shaker because it's the same day you replace your vacuum cleaner belt.

That all but forgotten fish tank in the attic is taken out, filled and checked for leaks every six months.

Your used golf balls are blazing white and smell suspiciously of a 10-day soak in industrial strength chlorine.

You know that fuzzy clump of grunge that collects in the folds of your floor shift boot? Of course, you don't – you're an Iowan. You clean that boot with Q-tips every week and then apply Armor All.

That faint suspicion of a grease spot on your garage floor has not actually surrendered to your weekly onslaught of Comet, bleach, Gunk grease solvent, and a floor sander, but it might as well.

When somebody puts a spice back in your rack out of alphabetical order, somebody is asked to say the alphabet just to make sure everybody is clear on the concept.

Any free range keys in drawers to unknown locks have long been rounded up, matched with locks, tagged and sequestered in a box clearly identified by your well-worn Label Maker Junior.

There are no dead insects in your light fixtures.

Your recipes are filed and no secret ingredients left out.

Iowans are, in Navy parlance, squared away and shipshape in Bristol fashion.

Virtue thy name is Iowa

In January of 1982 a reader signing herself only as "Debbie" asked:

"Are you still picking on Iowans?"

Now hold on a minute, Deb. I have never *picked on* Iowans, nor for that matter made disrespectful jokes about Hawkeyes that would hold up in court. I like to think that I have made several risible generalizations about Iowans based on laudatory hearsay. The truth is I have never met an Iowan I didn't want to hug and give some sugar. Iowans, I will say for the umpteenth time, are fine upstanding, warm, neighborly people, brimming with pioneer values, early to bed, starve a cold and stuff an orphan.

It is possible, Debbie, that at some time or another I have suggested that Iowans tend to be a trifle unexciting as in non-drama queens, and that is a good thing in my estimation.

No, wait, I'm fumfering here. I did say Iowans were unexciting back before I knew better. Iowans do tend to be unexcitable and there's a difference. I can illustrate with a county fair story out of the 1930s.

Suspended Aviation

A 1920s barnstormer with a war surplus bi-plane came to the county fair offering 10-minute flights around the pea patch. The family of a farmer known to be skeptical of flight were amazed when the old man agreed to go up for a spin.

So, the family chipped in, and the old fellow mutely allowed himself to be strapped in, and taken up for a gander at the countryside from 1,000 feet. When the airplane returned and taxied up to the waiting family 10 minutes later, the farmer hadn't so much as changed his expression.

"Well, Dad, this machine took you way up in the air and brought you safely back," the elder son said. "Now, were you flying or not?"

"Maybe I was," he conceded, "but I never did let my full weight down."

More reasons to love Iowa

Hospitals are 5-star: You can get tapioca 24/7. When you leave intensive care the nurses are nice as pie and make you promise to hurry back.

To an Iowan, a trip to the hospital in an ambulance is an adventure, and a chance to operate the siren.

Iowa is our only state with modest nudists. Sure, they go naked, but they wear nose glasses.

Iowa's liberalized drug laws no longer require a prescription for chicken soup.

Iowan dogs will decline food offered from the table, but you will feel the gratitude for the thought. Iowa dogs drink from the toilet, but they do remember to put the seat down. I've mentioned this before, but too remarkable not to repeat.

Iowa cats come when called. If guests overstay, they sleep on their faces. Yes, another repeat, but bordering on the miraculous and I choose to believe and remind.

Iowan blind date complaint: "You should have told me she was so pretty. I'd have worn my good cap."

After a tornado, Iowans like to go outside and sit on the nearest furniture and guess where they are. No, wait – BONG! BONG! BONG! – missplaced joke from the **Kansas** pile.

Iowan laws are strictly enforced. Bank robbers who pass a note to the teller get five years minimum with up to two years tacked on for bad penmanship.

Hitchhikers get rides, but they have to put up with a lecture on the dangers of hitchhiking. Drivers get scolded by the hitchhiker for picking up strangers.

Iowans are so straight-arrow they turn themselves in for running amber lights

On his death bed an Iowan husband confessed all to his sobbing wife. She was bored to tears.

Did you hear about the Iowa politician who scandalized his supporters at a fund raiser? He showed up with quiche on his breath.

I've noted earlier that some towns in Iowa are so small (Goldfield, pop. 700) that the phone book has a yellow paragraph. Towns in neighboring **Nebraska** are even smaller: one hoof towns before they rate as one horse towns.

MADE FROM SCRATCH IOWA PIG JOKE

A pig goes into a bar located a decent difference from the town limits of Goldfield, and says, "Somebody in here called me. What do you want?"

The bartender says, "Get out of here. We don't serve pigs here."

"Oh, really?" says the pig. "Then how come I heard someone from inside this bar call – sooooie, pig, pig, pig pig, you know, repeating pig, pig, pig?"

"Not me. Iowans don't repeat themselves." declares the barkeep.

"Well, somebody did and I can still hear him, only not so loud." The barkeep shrugs and glances away from the pig. "Maybe it's that drunken grizzly over there in the corner."

Sure enough, the bear is hunched over his beer mumbling "Sooooie, pig, pig, pig, pig, pig" without letup.

"What is he doing?" asks the pig.

"That bear's repeating."

FREE RANGE IOWA PALAVER

Iowans optimistic? They'll order the tuna surprise on Mondays.

Iowans are so darn pleasant that behind their backs Mormons call them "goody two-shoes".

And patient? Iowans are as patient as a sink full of dirty dishes.

Iowans keep Groucho nose glasses in the glove box and slip them on when they catch kids staring, then snatch them off before the parents can look.

Iowan gynecologists are very big on donning nose glasses just to break the ice with new patients.

Yes, there are plenty of overweight Iowans who could stand to lose a few. This is not a character defect or lack of willpower, but a fairness issue. When everyone has the same metabolism, chubby Iowans will stick to a diet.

Do Iowans remember to phone their mothers? Do nuns wear sensible shoes?

IOWA NICE VISITS FLORIDA

An Iowa woman on a shelling vacation on Florida's famous Sanibel Island picks up a magnificent trophy conch shell, and seeing an 8-year-old girl who is having no luck at all, suddenly puts the huge conch to her ear, saying "Hello?...Oh, yes, she's right here."

And then she hands the shell to the girl, saying, "It's the ocean calling. It's for you."

And with that, she leaves the little girl with the magnificent shell to her ear, and walks serenely down the beach in search of more shells.

Iowa praise gags one claiming to know one

A couple of decades ago, one newspaper reader was up to the gills with my treacly praise of Iowans, and wrote me a letter that told me a thing or two. I have honored her request for anonymity.

"I disagree with your glowing description of an Iowan – I married one. He cusses out every driver on the road. He believes that no one is going to heaven except those who belong to his special church.

"He thinks volunteering is foolish except for an occasional act of charity to the V.F.W. when he wants to offer. And he is contemptuous of Republicans, yuppies, rock bands, snow birds, beach lovers, and Floridians in particular. Where did you ever meet such saintly Iowans as the ones you describe?

Yours sincerely,

A well-traveled and hopefully tolerant citizen of the U.S.A.

Dear Well-traveled,

Are you sure you married an Iowan? My guess is that you were married to a man born in **Michigan** and reared by wolverines, or birthed in Wisconsin and nurtured by a wheel of cheese. By the time he was adopted by an Iowan couple – and here I surmise - it was too late.

Still, I will admit that I so cherish the idea that in these 50 states there is one state that got it right, and that I have probably subconsciously filtered out Iowa's seamier side. I have checked into it.

Iowa does have a seamy side that is always clean, starched and mended. Here are some things I have found out much to my chagrin.

Iowa has a reform school with one inmate. A fourth grader who attempted to sniff paste.

Iowans, like the rest of us, do occasionally get up on the wrong side of the bed. But when they do, they push the bad side against the wall so that it doesn't happen again.

The shame of the state is Instant Postum abuse. There is a hotline and clinics.

Iowa's suicide rate is so low as to be a statistical improbability. Despondent Iowans go into Baltimore restaurants where they are ignored to death.

Last year's top scandal was 11 state employees caught using the government WATS line for personal calls. They paid the money back, apologized for abusing the public trust and promised not to do it again.

An Iowan man invented the spork. He was summarily sent to Coventry. I'm not kidding. Iowan ill-wishers put him on a plane to England and told him not to return on pain of a sound pink-bellying.

In Iowa cigarette papers must carry a warning that smoking corn silk can cause coughing. Shoot, that was another misplaced joke from my **Illinois** file.

Gang fights in Iowa are a problem, but only on Halloween night when gangs of outhouse tipping teens clash with gangs of outhouse righting teens following in their wake.

Old joke, probable Iowa origin

Still and all, most Iowans are rigorously law-abiding and avidly married. Case in point was an Iowan house painter returning to a house where he had painted the bathroom the day before. No sooner had he gone into the house and set up for the day's work when the pretty woman who hired him wanted to show him how her husband had forgotten the wet paint warning and left a handprint.

"Come into the bathroom," she said brightly, taking his arm. "I want to show you where my husband put his hand last night."

"Uh, if it's all the same to you lady" stammered the painter, "couldn't we just split a beer?"

Near swooning reported

Are Iowans overly-excitable, or just easily entertained?

Feller named Jim Curtis of Muscatine, IA, writes the editor of the *Muscatine Onslaught Journal Intelligencer* about getting his arm autographed by Willie Nelson. The experience seems to have meant something to him. How I got the letter is, well, not remembered with perfect clarity.

Dear Editor

Willie Nelson autographed my arm. The next day I had it tattooed! After that the phone started ringing. I had calls from Los Angeles, Texas and several other states. The story was in the newspaper and on the radio. It was on three TV stations, CBS, NBC and CNN. It was the most exciting experience of my life.

Jim Curtis, Muscatine, Iowa

So what is a committed Iowa watcher like myself to do other than conclude that Iowans have a pretty low excitement threshold if one of their own declares that getting his arm signed by Willie Nelson was the most exciting experience of his life?

Again I am reminded that Iowans are blessed to grow up in an environment that heightens their sensitivity to experiences many of us are too darned preoccupied to appreciate. Iowans can teach us to wake up and smell the mimeograph ink. Evidence continues to mount that Iowans experience life more intensely than the bulk of us. Usually in a good way, but not always.

Iowans head for the lobby when it looks like Bambi will be a goner in the forest fire. They stormed the projection booth when the circus roustabouts abused Dumbo's mom.

Iowa Laundromats have an adult section with an R-rated dryer for diaphanous lingerie – you know what I'm talking about, scanties that wouldn't pad a crutch.

An Iowan doctor decided that he should give the bad news straight to his friend, a farmer. "Jim, I'm afraid you're going to get a visit from the Grim Reaper."

"Well, I'm awful fond of my International Harvester," the patient allowed, " but if the salesman is a friend of yours, I suppose I can sit still for a demonstration."

When finalists in the Iowa State Fair bran muffin bakeoff are announced, medics stand by with smelling salts at the ready and paddles charged.

An Iowan woman shot her husband after he poured ketchup on her hand-cranked peach ice cream. She was let off with a warning.

Excitement Kansas Style

If Iowans are easily entertained by small things, **Kansans** themselves are entertaining.

Only in Kansas do you hear somebody say, "Come here, Ed, and watch this fly bang himself against the window!"

In Iowa, they cure insomnia by looking at dictionary illustration. Kansans are a little different. Viewing dictionary illustrations gets them too keyed up to sleep.

Kansas aren't much given to boasting, but let one walk three miles of sidewalk without breaking his mother's back and you'll never hear the end of it.

Kansans love filling out forms. Want to make a Kansans' day? Tell him the questions continue on the other side.

Favorite pickup line at a Kansas bar is, "Hey, you want to play dead man's finger?"

Second most popular bar line is: "See, if I open up the church, you see all the people."

Curiously enough, Kansan men do remarkably well with Missouri women with this line: "Come over to my place, and I'll disappoint you beyond your wildest dreams."

A Kansan's idea of a cheap thrill is opening the raisin bran box from the bottom where the raisins have settled.

Kansans are beyond getting excited about tornados. When they want a mayonnaise jar opened, they just stick it out the window and wait a while.

Iowans reading the above should feel a little better now. Kansans a bit put upon, and if so, consider the source.

WILL IOWA TAKE A POWDER?

Back when the Soviet Union was unraveling, Lithuania seceded from the Soviet Union. At the time, I was afraid that the move to independence would give the State of Iowa ideas.

What if Iowa takes a good look at the rest of the union and asks to be excused for the rest of the century? I can imagine Iowa giving notice.

Can you imagine sending in troops to quell a non-insurrection in Des Moines? It would be embarrassing. Iowans would meet the invaders at the city limits with coffee and apple pan dowdy. The Iowa Legislature would pass a resolution encouraging Iowans to quarter the soldiers for free. Why in the blue-eyed world, you may ask, would Iowa even think about seceding from the union?

Because Iowans are an upgrade from the common herd

I've spent a half a life time collecting anecdotal reports on these honest folks and found them to be, well, people who would never dog-ear a book, always use their turn signals, check the blind spot before changing lanes, declare all their income, and vote yes on school bond issues. In a word, they are better citizens than the rest of us by just about any standard you could name.

They're not snooty about it either. My theory is that Iowans don't know they set the standard. At least not yet. When they do take a hard look at the mess the rest of us are leaving for somebody to clean up, look out. Well, not that they would make a fuss. Iowans were brought up too well to grouse or go elitist on us. My guess is that some elected official will sense of stirring of real discontent and propose a way out to the voters.

Iowa, the Envy of the Nation

The pitch might go something like this:

"My fellow Iowans, perhaps like myself, you have noticed that problems which once were federal in nature have become state responsibilities. Increasingly, Washington tells us that we must accept more responsibility for maintaining our roads, shoulder more of our education burden, look to our own resources when it comes to rebuilding our infrastructure, caring for our poor, sheltering the homeless, and treating the sick.

"And do you know what, my fellow citizens? We have done a bang-up job on our end. We not only take care of our own, we lead the nation in all standards by which civilizations are measured. On top of that, we pay more per capita to the federal government than any other state, and we receive less in return.

"Our literacy is among the highest in the nation. Seventy-four percent of our cars boast bumper stickers proclaiming their children as honor roll students. Our highways and bridges are the envy of the nation. We have cleansed our air and purified our rivers, streams and lakes. Indeed, we have done so much for ourselves without the help or interference of Washington, that one must ask: why Washington at all?

"Because, we respond as one, we are patriots, spiritual descendents of the heroes of Valley Forge. And yet, when we harken back to this country's birth, let us recall our ancestors' purpose in binding several states into an ' indivisible' whole, a more perfect union.'

"Well, lo and behold, folks– Iowans have became more perfect and the rest of the union is stumbling along behind and fading out of sight.

"I am not suggesting that we secede and declare our independence. Let the other states see that we have *succeeded* and recognize that we are independent, a people unto ourselves. Oh, we'll still pay our share of the common defense, but I think we've got the rest of it under control, thanks to the dithering of the last couple of administrations.

"Well, let's sleep on it, fellow Iowans, and if we do decide to become the United Counties of Iowa, let us remember that we will always be the best of neighbors with those other states. Maybe given a chance to become a little more like Iowa, the other 49 will want to join us in a few years and we can give 'em a big hug and say, 'What kept you so long?'"

HOSPITALITY IOWA STYLE

(Author's note: In spring of 1999 I asked readers of The Palm Beach Post to help me plan a cross-country RV adventure. Pearl Whyte, 83, invited me to stop by for dinner.)

GOLDFIELD, IA - A confession: My Mount McKinley or bust adventure was really an excuse to route my trip through Iowa. I have this thing for Iowans, an idealization recalling an America of ice cream socials, barn raisings, lusty voices raised in community sings, and men determined to marry a gal just like Doris Day - and succeeding.

Sure, I've teased Iowans. I've said Iowan kids are so easily entertained that they beg to stay up on laundry nights just to watch the spin cycle. I've even said that they are so law abiding - and sensitive - that each year several Iowans are hushed to death in public libraries. So when I asked readers to help plan my route, I ached for an Iowan letter. I got a doozie from 83-year-old Pearl Whyte, who visits her daughter and family in West Palm Beach a few months each year and saw my solicitations.

Pearl promised that if I would stop by Goldfield, Iowa, during my travels, she would treat me to a ham dinner and apple pie. "Nothing fancy," she wrote. I jumped at her offer and gave her fair warning.

It was late Saturday evening when I cruised up to 622 Water St. The porch lights burned brightly on the big two-story house built by her father-in-law in 1912. Pearl, as everybody in this farm community of 700 calls her, was waiting on the porch as she promised.

I'll be honest, my first sight of Pearl was unsettling. Was it a good idea for an 83-year-old woman to be jumping up and down on her porch in the middle of the night?

"Oh, you're here, thank goodness you're safely here at last," she exulted, hurrying across the yard to greet me.

Widowed five years ago, Pearl, like many aging citizens of Goldfield, lives alone in a home big enough for three families. In her case, that alone needs qualification. People come and go from her house all day. She knows everyone. Family, friends from church, her coffee club, the choral group, the garden club and the occasional recommended stranger have the run of the place.

Whether she's there or not. "Nobody locks their house in Goldfield," Pearl explained.

Folks don't take their keys out of their cars, either. Too inconvenient. You'd just have to put them back in again, right? Unfortunately, on a half dozen occasions, this touching trustiness has turned Pearl Whyte into a noted car thief.

"Oh, no, don't tell him about the cars!" wails Pearl to her daughter, Maureen Cameron, who, with husband Lyle, is joining us for Sunday dinner. And Maureen, of course, doesn't tell me. At least not until she can stop laughing and catch her breath.

"In town, Mother just gets into any old red car and drives home. She usually figures it out, though, and gets back before they miss it."

And if the mistake isn't discovered, the owner just drives Pearl's car for the day. "One time," gasps Maureen, wiping back tears, "Mother says, 'Hey, whose groceries are these in the back of my car?'"

Folks around Goldfield don't generally drive fancy cars, so the presence of a big car or van in front of an established citizen's house often means a relative has been called in. If neighbors didn't read about a visiting son or daughter in the *Eagle Grove Eagle*, they want to know why.

"Neighbors are concerned if they see that unfamiliar car," says Scott Whyte, president of the local bank and cousin to Pearl's late husband, Conger. "They'll call and ask if anything's wrong."

Dinner was served, and after grace was said, we tucked into what witnesses agreed was as savory a ham dinner as has ever been served in these parts, and that's saying something. For dessert we had what in Goldfield is known as "Pearl's Apple Pie." Good? I scraped away the ice cream to get at the crust and filling.

When Lyle Cameron let on that I was being built up to experience Pearl's fudge, I couldn't imagine fudge with a reputation. What made it special?

"It's just evaporated milk, cocoa, sugar and butter," Pearl shrugged, "but I beat it by hand for two hours, sometimes just an hour if it sets up."

I will confess I had every intention of eating my ham dinner, setting a spell as we say in the South, then rambling on to Wind Cave National Park in South Dakota for spelunking, as another contributor to my itinerary had suggested. However, when I learned that spelunking doesn't start until June, I found myself wanting to hang out with Pearl.

I probably looked at more photographs than anybody would ordinarily sit still for, but I saw pictures of a graduation dress and nine family members who wore it in their turn. I saw photographs of the Ford dealership founded by Pearl's father-in-law in 1914, back when they simply called it the Ford garage. If you wanted a Model T, you ordered it and picked it up at the garage. If it needed fixing, George Whyte fixed it.

I asked Pearl so many questions about her life that she finally handed me a collection of her memories of growing up in the metropolis of Eagle Grove - population 7,000 - five miles east of Goldfield.

Born May 22, 1916, Pearl Stella Hovland came too late to live in the chicken coop where Peter and Sophie Hovland lived while building a homestead. She survived whooping cough as an infant and recalls a two story house with no plumbing or electricity, but a cistern and pumps.

The Hovlands had cows, chickens, pigs and 33 acres planted with oats, corn, vegetables, apples, potatoes, peas, carrots and grapes. Everything was cooked and canned. Peter Hovland delivered mail.

"We butchered our own beef and pork," she wrote. "That sounds better than cows and pigs."

In the morning, milk was delivered to neighbors by the children as Peter drove the Model-T. Night deliveries were dreaded, especially in zero weather: "Dad would come up from the basement with the milk carrier in his hand and say 'Have I got any runners? Who will run tonight?"

Pearl recalls that some customers could pay and some couldn't. Curiously, Peter favored those who couldn't pay, throwing in a dozen eggs or a pint of cream every so often. "His reasoning was valid. Those that could pay could buy eggs and cream . . ."

At age 7, Pearl lost her mother, who died from complications following childbirth. Despite the sorrow, Pearl recalls a childhood full of music and work, and a resourceful, loving father who went on to endear himself to his children and his community.

One of her most cherished memories is of a Christmas in which her dad brought in a fresh tree and glorified it with candles, each clamped onto its branch tip. Then Peter lit every one.

"I was spellbound. The tree glowed for a couple of minutes, then Dad put each out slowly. Oh God, if we could give our kids a moment of ecstasy like that!"

As I write this, I suspect Pearl Whyte hasn't a particle of an idea how many lives she has touched with her exuberant good cheer and her loving spirit. We stopped by the post office where everyone in Goldfield picks up their mail, and she couldn't get out of the place before a man who had known her 30 years ago rushed up and said, "Hey, Pearl, how about some of that apple pie?"

That was Roger Griffith, visiting from California and recently retired from airline flying, swinging by the old neighborhood.

"How on earth did he recognize me after all these years?" she wondered.

I was going to ask if she recalled the former resident stopping by the house to retrieve his car, but decided Pearl had been teased enough for one weekend.

HOW HANDSOME WAS MY LAMB

Once upon a news from Lake Woebegone, Minnesotan Garrison Keillor tells a childhood story of boys tossing pebbles at penned pigs and how the farmer blew his stack. The pigs deserved better.

That bit of Midwestern perspective was brought home to me by an Iowan newspaperman I met some years ago at a columnists' meeting in Louisville. Five of us, four columnists from lesser states, and our Iowan, found ourselves poring over a menu that was very odd indeed. The meat dishes were described – well, in rather lurid detail. I'm serious. What follows was inspired by the menu of the Normandy Inn quoted verbatim.

LOUISVILLE, KY – It was wet and raw and after three days of virtual house arrest, five members of the National Society of Newspaper Columnists struck out for a restaurant, any restaurant, so long as it sprang us from the hotel.

Hardly had we taken a chill and run a temperature when we chanced upon the Normandy Inn and found ourselves studying the menu, a remarkable document as bills of fare go. I had never seen food assigned human qualities.

Neither had Daryl Dimple of the *Des Moines Vague Rumor*. "My goodness," he said, "I can't order the 'Le Canard a l'orange curacao'. I think it was somebody's pet."

"What are you talking about?" asked Charlie Robbins of the *Tampa Times*, his finger on the menu item. "'Roasted duckling, quite plump, flamed at your table.'"

"A baby duck, quite plump?" repeated the Iowan. "I think I'm going to be sick. I can't watch some child's Easter duck set on fire on my plate."

"Well, then,Daryl," ventured Steve Mitchell, columnist for the *Palm Beach Evening Independent,* "perhaps you should stay clear of this 'English-cut tenderloin of flawless beef', unless of course, we can bribe the waiter to bring you a more worldly animal with a less savory past."

"You can joke," Daryl said, "but I won't eat food with character references. The quite plump duck and the flawless beef are out."

Skimming down the menu, I couldn't resist getting in on the fun. "Well then, so much for your 'robust heavy steer broiled to your pleasure in the approv'd manner,' I quoted. "I don't see how in good conscience you could eat a robust heavy steer struck down in the prime of life. Probably had plans for college."

A mirthless laugh escaped John Kelso of the *Austin American-Statesman*. "Then you'll probably pass on the 'baked fillet of baby halibut'. I'll bet they tore that little sucker screaming from its mother's breast for your dining pleasure."

Our Iowan blanched and then went greenish gray. I resisted suggesting that the baby halibut probably came with a baby rattle clutched in its tiny fin. There is such thing as piling on. Daryl's tormentors, myself excepted, were still scanning the menu for anthropomorphic entrees with big, soulful eyes. Mitchell dropped down to the final item and tossed another dart.

"Make up your mind, Hawkeye. You've still got 'veal cutlets most tender, appropriately broiled" and get this, 'young tender lamb, *quite handsome,* slowly roasted.' I earnestly entreat you, Daryl, to drop this unmanly squeamishness and order the handsome lamb. Otherwise this animal has thrown away a promising modeling career for naught."

"You guys go ahead and eat," Daryl said. "I think I saw some Cheez-Doodles back in the hospitality suite."

Indeed, our animal lover looked like he was about to make a run for porcelain. It was Kelso who ended the sport by summoning the waiter.

"Garçon!" Kelso snapped, bringing the waiter with the speed of an ox-drawn tumbrel.

"Is there a problem?" the waiter asked with the mildest of interest.

"Yes. Our Iowa friend here has an unusual fondness for domestic animals, and will not taste the flesh of charming, handsome, babyish animals of sterling character. Unless you can convince us that the establishment has exaggerated their virtues, he said, tapping the menu, "we shall take our custom elsewhere."

"I quite understand, sir," said the waiter, adopting a confidential tone. "The fact is, we were expecting new menus today and there have been substitutions."

"Such as?" Kelso inquired.

"The robust heavy steer was in fact a sullen animal given over to every species of riot and debauchery. Animal Control paid us $50 to put the brute down. The roasted 'duckling' was 15 years old if he was a day, and lived out of the dumpster of an Asian buffet until he got into the dining room and put a child's eye out.

"The flawless beef was wanted for mopery in Kansas," the waiter continued tonelessly. "The young tender lamb, quite handsome, was handsome all right. He spent his formative years in the towel room of the Christian Seafarers' Athletic Club in Kowloon and was named in an alienation of affections action involving..."

"Enough!" the Texan said. "What's the story on the baby halibut?" We were distracted by a commotion from the kitchen

"By the sound of it," replied the waiter glancing towards swinging doors, "that would be him drowning the sauce chef in the live tank."

I don't think Daryl heard a word of it, absorbed as he was by the vegetarian option. He finally ordered the glazed carrots and a cup of tea. The rest of us ordered the Handsome Lamb. Figured he had it coming.

Reader Challenge!

Can you write an upbeat joke that celebrates Midwestern values? If so, send your original observation that pokes gentle fun at the Iowans and near-Iowans you have come to know and love. We'll pick the best for Iowa Nice II and make you famous well within your wildest dreams. For entry forms and more books by Ron Wiggins, go to:

www.iowanice.com

7287503R0

Made in the USA
Charleston, SC
13 February 2011